RESTING PLACE OF SURVIVAL

poems by Gianella Ghiglino

© 2025 copyright Jaded Ibis Press

First Edition. All rights reserved.

Printed in the USA. No part of this book may be used or reproduced in any manner without written permission from the publisher, except in the case of brief quotations embodied in critical articles or reviews. For information, please email: info@jadedibispress.com.

ISBN: 978-1-938841-33-0
ESBN: 978-1-938841-34-7

Cover and interior book design: Nicole Roberts
Cover art illustration: Nicole Roberts

This book is available in paperback and electronic book formats.
Ghiglino, Gianella

Resting Place for Survival / Ghiglino

CONTENTS

Immigrant	1
Blessing	2
Qantu	3
For Us	4
Limeña	5
Broken Spanish	6
Chola	8
"El Indio no Llora."	9
The Long Drives	10
Marcara	11
Homelands	12
Las Calles	13
Becoming	14
The Dilemma	15
I Don't Write about Rape	16
Blue Shutters	17
Legacy	18
Randa's Poem	19
The Conversation after the Argument	20
Things I Am Afraid to Tell Them	21
10/11/2020	22
The Man from Venezuela	24
Forgiveness	25
To Love Again	26
That Night	27
Grace	28
Home	29

Dance with the Ancestors	30
Evening Wishes	31
Rooted	32
During Panic Attacks	33
Ode to the Andes	34
Lovers	35
Acceptance	36
The Valley	37
8/24	38
Mothers of Forced Sterilization	39
Forgiving God	41
RE: Frost	43
Generational Trauma	44
Raymi	45
The Odds	46
I Come from Storytellers	47
New Year's Eve	48
Grieving the Living	49
Herlinda	50
In Time	51
Llamellín	52
Lessons from the Shaman in Cusco	53
A Birth	54
Descriptions	55
The New Age	56
How to Re-frame the Breakup	57
Amar	58
Choice	59
The Most Important	60

All the Best	61
History	62
Behind the Apartment	63
Leaning	64
Effort	65
Advice	66

Para mis padres quien me enseñeron a ser valiente.

For Carlo and Olga, who taught me I am not bound by the chaos that brought me here but by the brilliance that came out of it.

Immigrant

Borders are very much like collectors
Holding on to rosaries, wallet-sized families, and sometimes
    people
I was draped in white, an enemy in foresight
I collected pieces of trauma and hung them like ornaments.
    Devotion, I said, I call this exhibit *Devotion.*
Rain, you become rain unwanted unless there is a drought.
I hold my arms to my chest; body heat might calm the heart.
    The carcass of home slipping off with every step.
The moon will eventually make an appearance to say: I am here,
    and I am all you have.
Flowers sprout on wooden houses to say: you have inherited my
    pulse.
The marrow of the earth thickens and leads the way.
The way I am mining hope, I must have made peace with this
    land, even the land separating us.

Blessing

Grandmothers can give us peace that mimics the earth's
  embrace
Her fear guarded her
She went looking for a blessing.
To become an immigrant, undone stitchings in movement. A
  flower clipped of its livelihood.
To become a shadow without flesh
The breeze on a hot day that goes ignored
To become anything but human
To be but a name only *enunciated* correctly through a long-
  distance call.

Qantu

I ask what it is like to be brave

To confide in an instinct, waning deserts
To put all your hopes in one country—
To bid your entire history, mountain plains accustomed to your regard.

I ask what it takes to be brave

She responds with gold rising off her tongue
You have to be hopeful, tangled strands of doubt urging you to stay afloat and still, you mouth hope with your hands angled toward safety.

Like the qantu before it blooms, reckoning its message
with the divine
You have to have hope
Skies become the most sacred when you approach darkness like fog.

Only then do they begin to resemble something earthly. Hope becomes less of a question and more of a choice.

For Us

There is more they left us.
Far more than the war we never agreed to
We inherited the orchids
The softness in our palms
Intuition carved in our breath
We were never meant to wash away
To use the soap to scrape skin dull
Instead, bathe in our greatness
Spread the basil
Pour the mint
Soak in the flowers
Embrace the gifts in the kitchen
The steam of a recipe that brings lovers together
What if tragedies did not survive into the morning?
They would break at sunrise
Becoming a ruin by dawn
Collapse   at   the   sight   of   our
   refusal   to   settle   our   fortitude.

Limeña

Boleros, he said, that is how I fell in love. I bought the orchestra a round of beers. Our song crept into our ears like sunshine at the sight of daylight savings. I held her hand and swept her into my chest.

Lima sky, in all of its gloom, had never been that shade of blue. I whispered the lyrics into her ears until her eyes began to gleam with love. The right woman will do that to you; pull the weakness out and make you confront your doubt.

Boleros, he said, that is how I fell in love. And when I see her again en el alumbre de la muerte, le pediré un baile más.

Broken Spanish

When my dad calls there is a silence. A language sheltered in
    shame
I forget how to say *I love you* in Spanish   He says,
    it is ok
Bonds aren't held together by words
He doesn't know I splintered
My tongue at the age of nine when they said, speak English;
    you're in America.
I thought if I diluted Spanish into transparency
Took its verb apart from its nouns
Let them wander into oblivion
I'd be the American dream, its promise incarnate
But now I run and run, broken in half, trying to meet in the
    middle. I am angry
For the language that buried an accent in their throats
For international money orders that did not always arrive in
    time for surgery
For the graveyard shifts that became underlying conditions
For the goodbye that could only travel through a landline
For the lives they lost chasing survival in this one
I am sad
I don't understand the punchline of the joke
The lyrics of the song are proverbs I never learned
I can't tell him my dreams because I don't know the translation
    of my job title
I pause
He says, *have you eaten?*
An affirmation of love wrapped in a question
I describe what I ate and how I cooked it

I recite it like a prayer.

At this moment, I realize "home" is a feeling that persists even when you don't.

Chola

Morena pero bonita
Los cholos, los indios son feos
My beauty does not come from metastasized blood, making a
    scarcity of my people.
My beauty comes from prayers in Quechua
Songs for Inti on the quena
Mi abuela de piel morena en Aczo
In her eyes, you can see the entire city's landscape
A picturesque promise of God's ingenuity
My beauty comes from flushed cheeks of roses ascending with
    pride
From Apu, the earth's oath to always rise
Brown skin is a page in history, opulent in theories and practices
It does not fold or wrinkle; it is incandescent in daylight
The beauty of my people is undeniable.

"El Indio no Llora."

I've come to terms with tears, the tears that spread like a disease. They say the "Indian" does not feel or cry—survival wrapped in the spine. Bones curdle in defeat in the depression that is never acknowledged. I have spent years straightening my pride—tears in my eye ducts, repression of something vital. **I** have pleaded with my sadness to exist outside of me. I tell it "el Indio no llora." The crimes unfold in my body, fleeting recognition of these organs. I replete myself as a "donor" to give this hunger to someone else. The only survival I have known is hiding.

If you hide long enough, you learn to hear the world in mumbles, making meaning of the slightest infractions. "El Indio no llora." No tears have ever been exposed to the heaving of sunlight, blushing away old skin. No tears understand the race to **my** neck, a cave securing secrets. No tears understand survival like the ones that never leave. "El Indio nunca llora."

The Long Drives

Each mile becomes a conclusion.
A dichotomy of how the human heart measures grief by
    distance and not time
I let the music become the narrator.
Headlights guide me somewhere while the sadness flushes out
    of me in increments.
I grieve like my dad
On drives that are supposed to be grocery runs.

Marcara

The air was different in La Sierra.
Each time you walked up the hill by the bridge, the mountains granted you another inch, another breath
The smell of earth and pavement rustled together, as if in a ceremony pledging bliss to Mother Earth
The eucalyptus leaves on the mercado floor gathered impressions
The bread at the bakery rose
The coca leaves chewed as taxi drivers started another day
I thought of how you never returned
How hometowns can become folk stories at dinner tables
How even after forty years, you emphasized each syllable in her name
Carried her stride across continents
Taught me that pride was implicit, as you traced the creases on the palm of my hand.

Homelands

There is something about bringing a lover home.
Bringing a lover to what I could have been
I tell you, this is my home.
My entire being meditates on this view
These mountains breathe life into a sanctuary
The sun eases an elopement that reigns indefinitely
I want you to love this land as I have
In the months between vacations
In the stories my mom loves to repeat
The food my dad swears is the best in the world
Machu Picchu is adorned with my pride
I want you to love this land as I have
The distance I created, I am still folding away.

Las Calles

There are tragedies stored in my blood
Too dismal, too foreign to feel like my own
Pain engraved on trees like two lovers' names who no longer
    speak
I exist like the stem of bruised fruit
Asking for the weight to be cut loose
There are men wearing skins that resembles mine
Wearing deceit with pride
The clicks of locks on doors
The creak of the bed on the second floor
They were all just little girls
Their silence transcends generations
Like cold pavement waiting for the sun to rise
Surviving is not betrayal

Becoming

Women in my lineage have survived centuries of abuse from men who told them love resembled betrayal. My mother survived a country that promised her hope but did not tell her that she would break when she made a long-distance call home.

My father survived a country that swallowed his dignity with every English word he could not pronounce. And yet, I am doubting if I can survive your loss, as if I have never shattered into the stratosphere and returned brighter and more whole. And you are just another poem that my mouth has to spit out.

I cannot doubt my resilience. It is the most concrete thing I possess.

My whole life has been one revival after another.

The Dilemma

After the assault, I swore I was fine
I even contemplated calling the police
At least, I thought for a second that I deserved some "justice." I didn't call
Not because I didn't think they would believe me
But because they would
Because he was of my complexion, my ethnicity
How do you ask for help in a place that does not want you? In a city where time holds still, where the past belongs to the present
I couldn't do that
I wouldn't do that because we all exist as one. We fall together
And the "good immigrant narrative" will only give us a lifeline for so long.
Our complexities, our differences, and our intentions are insignificant to them.
My blood has sown with yours.
Our progress depends on how we scorn the devil's advocate
At night, I am a prayer in line, waiting to be heard.
Ready to bargain the most intimate parts of myself I wish I didn't have, to protect you
If only the ocean could become the sky
If only the crow could become the hummingbird
If only the stars could wish back
If only justice were more than good intentions.

I Don't Write about Rape

I've spent years searching for my memories, as if my body is not aching with the truth. It wasn't a dream I couldn't remember or a day I blacked out.
The bruise on my leg would not wash away in the boiled water. It was real, but I do not write about rape.
And when I lay their memories to rest, it's not because I wish to forget.
I refuse to create a story out of that
I refuse to find vivid descriptions and comparisons. I refuse to try and appeal to humanity.
As if I am breaking bread in hell, promising heaven can come from this
I don't write about rape.
Instead, I let my body know it was not my fault.
It was not at any age, bust size, income, or even blood alcohol level.
It was never my fault
The worst part is pretending it was not that bad
To rationalize symptoms you can't explain or gashes, you cannot hide
And with those memories, I lay that truth to rest
Their shame was never my burden to hold
To carry through the schoolyard or work
As I let the details fade, I remember I don't write about rape because who would want to read a poem about that?

Blue Shutters

For too long, women who look like me have evoked images of healing
Collapsed bridges and scaffolds have led to entitled prophecies
Too often left behind until we believe it
And we always will until we stop aspiring to whiteness
Whiteness as a metaphor and whiteness as a savior
I learned to say my name even when my tongue was carrying pillars
I learned to hold my breath without losing it
I learned to walk upright into obscurity
I learned how fear is not the martyr of success
Love is the plea between moments and eternity
Nights reign celestial forthcomings
Mornings strike a light boundless of their salute. This grace is also our pursuit.

Legacy

Hunger, she said. I refuse to let you inherit hunger
You will never know what it's like to inhale air and pretend it is
    food
You will never know what it's like to do your homework by the
    lamppost
Or go to the mercado to work before your age has two digits
The uncles that like to touch little girls will never be able to lure
    you with apple juice.
I held her strength in my gaze,
She said, your dreams are proof I gave you the best of mine
The day I said, *I do.*
The first brick your dad laid under a half-eaten sun in Los
    Olivos
The day your sister held you in her arms for the first time
The day your hands wrapped my finger, life dawning a divinity
    only we recognize
You are my legacy, a prayer that exists as a vow.

Randa's Poem

Death is not as equal as it advertises.
I huddle my dreams and promises and tell them to forget you,
    not to expect you.
Wounds denounce pain—a numbness ensues. The remnants of
    yesterday's struggle
Through the saltwater of grief that only knows how to rust,
    I seek words for you
You have taught me that love is simple,
Friendship occurs in the stillness, in the space that receives light
    unconditionally.
A grounding that establishes an element
The concept of forever is everything I inherit from my
    ancestors. There aren't enough delicate places in a poem to
    place you
I pull my eyes up to the sun to dry them. I miss you,
    I whisper in unison.

The Conversation after the Argument

I leave my comfort in the couch cushions, tangled in between words. Tongues roping together *what-ifs* and *I-should-haves*. The walls are discreet in their judgment. Crooked light fixtures remind us of what we need to fix. I leave my pride aside. Leave my words to filter through. To gauge in peace, in reconciliation. I am fixated on the idea of "needs." The needs we have, the needs we create to be heard. We arch our wrists backward to hold each other's hands. I remember my grandpa's words the night I asked him how to make love last. "If people were simple, love would be, too, but they're not. You yield with caution, but you continue to move."

Any direction you keep on.

Things I Am Afraid to Tell Them

1. I needed you at the ages of four, eleven, seventeen.
2. The days I resorted to writing, I found words I never heard from you.

3. I know it was not your choice.
4. Choices are privileges that do not tend toward survival.
5. Survival is crouching over a pregnant belly in pitch black. Cities fall in flames: our land stifled in tragedy.
6. They later called it "Fujimorismo."

7. We found our way out.
8. I became a tangent apology: carrying forgiveness as a peace offering for existing.

9. The land of dreams was always an expert at taking them. I never told anyone, and survival is finite.

10. The scope of resilience is measured in skin tones. Memories are belongings, even the bad ones are a sacred communion. Their heartbreak and mine, a composite of hope.
11. Only then do we find why silence, when welcomed, is the most tender.

10/11/2020

I'll never know what those five days were like for you
Each day is worse than the last
Lungs hardening into oblivion
Nurses come into your room faceless
You wonder if she's scared she'll catch it
Wrapped in plastic
It's airborne; it's the droplets, and here you are, fading into it
They say there's no medicine, no money from the state
You feel your heart let go
Etching a goodbye
Your mind says, let's calm down and listen to some music
A bolero maybe
They don't allow radios or visitors, and you are barely allowed to breathe
Your heart begins to count to 1, 2, 3
Each number gets longer
Stretching between hope and reality
The brain says, a ventilator, that's what we need—more oxygen
But there aren't ventilators for people like you
For those who have collected decades and have seen the best and worst of humanity
For the poor, the sacrificed, the comorbidities
You always told me you weren't afraid of death
That death is our final gift
Rest is a declaration of love
1, 2, 3, 4, your heart says, and 5 takes the last sigh
For you, prayers will break even and vow intent
For you, oceans will bow themselves to peace

I'll grieve the body that housed you and finally cry about what
   we've been surviving
I'll see you, I'll see you, I'll see you again.

The Man from Venezuela

He told me the rainforest is terrifying. Claiming lives without discernment
A land that originates folklores
The alchemist that sprouts forests from its chest
The myths of the world, the good and the bad, endure in her purpose
I see the Amazon as a place of healing
Expressing revenge to those that bring it destruction
And giving meaning to those who protect her from a bounty
A place that binds to you
Like water searching for whom to nourish
Divinity meeting a blissful isolation
He told me it is strange how we can both become the memory of land, but only one of us had to walk through it.

Forgiveness

No one tells you how surviving it all is just the beginning
How the worst days of your life will be the ones that follow
The days I thought I could not survive
How the body grips the memories like a rosary prayer
How bathroom floors ground you as you count your fingers
How running water becomes a mediation for lost thoughts
How your throat cages the body, promising a sanctuary
How the heart loses belief and creates idols of all the hurt
How does healing find its place when you're the one misguiding it? When did nature over nurture become my apathy?
Surviving is what happens first. Every day you begin
Healing is a place of forgiveness
It's a place of praise
Each part displayed in honor
Holding the breath in comfort until it returns home
There is beauty in how we survive, how the best of us is yet to exist

To Love Again

Love does not happen again or the same.
The best love occurs when the torn accentuates the mend
The ease we long for never returns
Instead, it nurtures the gratitude that coexists with the past
Love does not come in cycles
It does not regard time as a composer
Nor blinds the future with shards begging to be together
Instead, love is
Like unexpectedly catching a sunset and giving it the grace to descend
A beginning that is simple enough to feel familiar
Yet, it is a love that exists entirely for the present
For the version of you that decides to try again
The ease will come; it transforms with us
And with it, a release of the longing we once had.

That Night

He said he loved me for the first time
The night my grandpa was dying
I like to think he tapped my boyfriend's shoulder and said, go ahead
Find the silver lining now, because tomorrow morning is going to feel infinite
When that call comes, she'll wither into herself in secret
She'll harden like the flesh of a pomelo
Every *what-if* and *why* will surface
She will bury her thoughts in your chest and paint them on your t-shirt.
The guilt of loving you while grieving me
As if elements can only exist in a singular form
The grief, the love, the certainty of both
The nuance of being
The songstress is nostalgia
I love you, he said in the silver lining.

Grace

We exchange childhood stories.
As if we are two different flowers in a garden learning to be
You tell me how wars leave wounds that never scar
How the dust of copper sinks into the skin, claiming scars
I tell you how the word *illegal* claims your dignity discreetly
How one day you wake up and the luster of your voice has
    slipped beneath your feet
You tell me how success can transform trauma
How the diplomas and dollars secrete enough moisture to be
    rubbed on all the cuts
I tell you how I forged an entire sky, brought stars into
    existence, and called them possibilities.
How, even still, it was not enough.
To be pulled out of poverty, to shed the skin of *low-income*. To
    carry the badge of sacrifice, an irrefutable potency
We search for something intrinsic
Perhaps even the most innate feelings can dissolve
You tell me that perhaps some wars end when you no longer
    hold on to the rubble
When you no longer search for your reflection in the debris
I tell you how maybe dignity is not the source of loss
Not a place of loss
Loss is a lack of memory
And even the victories exist within us.

Home

In Caraz, they say
The peak of the day when the ocean and sky meet
The moment they become endless
That union is love
When I'm with you, I'm convinced love can heal ancestral
 wounds
I break into a dialect that is earned
Becomes each word that isn't allowed to be spoken
Becomes the legacy of a stolen past
The density of bones buried under gold churches
The wind that guides our daughters left
The saints given to us for each part of our journey
The rain that washes away footprints as they carry the casket
 around town
The bark of the tree that mends and mends
When I'm with you, I'm convinced
Love has always been my inheritance.

Dance with the Ancestors

I dream of coming home to you
In songs
In the spirit
Swept winds caressing the Rio Santo that washed away our sorrow
They say love is eternal, the semblance of everything we have, everything we touch.
I dream of coming home to you
I'll confess how there is a part of me that is afraid to be happy
You tell me how there are things the Spaniards could never destroy
From the destruction, the worship ascends
Healing is a passage acquired from the water, accepting us wholly. Huachuma was never meant to be understood by them.
Enlightenment is a gift; it was never our curse.
It was never the devil they saw spawn from our mountains
It was always the reflection from their gun barrels
It was never the gold that mattered, never the gold that kept us arisen
Never about the gold they stole, never about the gold they murdered for
Soiled holy houses cannot welcome God
It has always existed in us
We are north and south
You are the sun
I am the moon
El cóndor que pasa
Together, we'll fly through the brisk afternoon.

Evening Wishes

On the nights the sky looks like it did, I think about how the
    light of the moon
Lit us into tomorrow
Eased us into the sunrise
Arriving at the chance to be renewed.

Rooted

Nature is healing for a reason.
We are all borrowed soil and water
From sunrises avowing stems that spring holy
Our bodies sustain the earth's memories
In the end, when we return to the land,
We will grant life again,
Becoming the vibrancy that occurs in seasons
Giving rise to lakes that nourish
Being rooted and blessing the next breaths
We were always vessels of healing
What reigns over more truth, more beauty than that?

During Panic Attacks

He ran the bathwater. Burned the palo santo
Steeped the tea
Guided my breath home like it was his own,
I wish I could tell twenty-year-old me
That lovers that love do exist
That you do not need to search for reasons to stay
Instead, reasons watch you in plain sight, marveling at what is
What a life, they whisper among each other
Fear resembles love in intensity
But only one can live in a state of consistency, I wish I could tell twenty-year-old me
The distinction between what is inherent and acquired will get lost for a while
But what is love, if not radical—an embrace that celebrates it all.

Ode to the Andes

In the sacred temple of the moon, we watched the flames rise in respite, taking our offerings beyond.

I began to think of the way my mom calls me Yuyu
In Quechua, that means "herb," a funny thing to call a child, but as

I stood in awe, smoke creased and shaped with the wind

I thought of how the words I associated with love
Came from a language that survived, a bond solidified by the rapture of time
Consumed by the heat emitted by my ancestors' intent
To stand alongside the earth and ask for forgiveness for wounds

I did not cast.
Bringing defiance to its knees
Eyes poised in agreement
Gratitude brings us home, where lovers go to make faithful wishes
Evenings shuffle night stars into familiarity
To exist amid, in spite
A miracle in its glory
That is enough, a moment living as a verse
Everything I associate with love, coming from lessons engrained
The day I return to the earth
Let my life be a reminder; gratitude is an act of service
When indigenous blood spilled through our cities by force
The river valleys, the desserts, and the coastal soil began to flourish.

Lovers

She softly whispered, I love you.
Through the cold corridor where the hardwood floor creaked in harmony
Through a cracked sidewalk baring the proof of a capricious earth
Through the wind as it slipped in between window panels that blinked in reverence
It traveled and traveled
Until it reached you
The glory of every *I love you* begins where it ends.

Acceptance

Being loved by you, I learned to forgive
I learned to forgive the past for stealing the exhale of the present
I learned to forgive God for the things I prayed to forget
For the nights that crashed into my bedroom floor and just left
I found forgiveness in survival; in the poems, I had no choice
    but to write
In the showers that said, let me drain your grief
The hesitation before every *I'm good*.
Being loved by you, I learned that peace is a place of arrivals
That it lives in the details,
In the joke, my mother said last week
The hem your grandmother fixed
The playground that leaves my niece's braids loose
The excitement in your voice when you tell me about your
    dreams
My arrival, each time, becomes a new beginning.

The Valley

In the apartments that do not run credit checks, walls separate immigrant families learning to forget countries they trace on the tiny mounds of the stipple ceiling.
Half-finished stories promising to deliver a premise
Broken branches searching for trees to cling to as they scope the pavement-suppressing roots
The etymology of words lost in pronunciation
You learn to find reasons to belong
Celebrating small wins like memorizing the route from school to home
Supporting the home team and cheering for championships because sports feel like neutral ground
Finding your flag waving at the car dealership as if its banter with the wind is a salute to you
Throwing away the dollar bills from back home, knowing time will be the only currency that will bring you closer
Becoming more like the men in your family, only breaking in the presence of God
Hands molded by red clay and emboldened by the mountain slopes that lead to the ocean
The day you return to your homeland as a visitor, you will realize the earth memorializes routes, your trajectory an expression of a country yearning to be free.

8/24

When the city sleeps, our dreams gather to commend you
A vigil of words, an embalmed sea stretches over us,
Envisioning a world where you live on
Convenience store walls belong to you, turning street corners into memorials
The children who know you, living through collective grief
To become a home with the pride of a country
The immigrant families find solace when you win championships
In the pickup games at the park that persists with ambition at the forefront
The dad with a few words, who only knows how to bond with his son through watching you play
The children you inspire to be better become just that
And the day you return to visit, we'll light a candle solely for you
A flame that flickers with distinction
We will carry you home.

Mothers of Forced Sterilization

Our minds are gracious in letting us experience what we will
     never know.

She held her fantasies close.
Gave them names, decorated town squares.
Each time a new detail would emerge.
At times it was patching up a bloody knee from the
     neighborhood soccer game.
Other times it was the soup boiling over laughter that sealed the
     room.

She entered in and out of those daydreams
High-pitched voices swiveled in and out of made-up
     conversations. Thoughts washed into memories
Weaving a smile met with questions
The irony is she never even wanted to become a mother
Never dreamt of life entering her body

Now her curiosity perches every time she sucks in her stomach.
     She wonders if that is what a kick would feel like
Perhaps in another life, the brown faces they deemed unworthy
     of living are doing just that.

In another life, she is patching up a bloody knee, pumping
     soccer balls to fullness.
She is making soup and adding the lentils to the broth.
Singing songs to awaken the day. Brushing black hairs away
     from brown eyes.
A sight of longing,

If consolation can only come in dreams, I see why they say death is the final embrace.

Forgiving God

To think my life is a prayer embodied,
Yet the last time I assumed a position of faith
I looked to the universe as a bushel of stories
    withering lessons

How do you trust a god that does not recognize your mother's
    tongue?
I look to the moon-seeking water in return for prosperity
Does peace accompany God? If so, why does fear follow
    intently? Flowing into currents, making shrouds of our
    rivers
Shaming the earth as she creeps into submission
Scolding eyes feeding off of the lowest fruit, claiming it a sin
The whispers of devils conjuring genocide
Is this Catholic guilt?
Can I find God in the church-crushing bone marrow?

She said, I crossed the desert, I heard God point me to the
    right; the pocketbook holy bible was the only thing I had
    left.
On his deathbed, he described the ending as a relief uniting him
    with the love of his life.
The man whose spine had taken the shape of cement street
    corners swore Jesus loved him.
Perhaps, the worst of it was never your aspiration

I look to the sky; blue rises to perfection, pursuing humility
Gravity solidifies peace in its place
Letting anger go, strand by strand

In that stillness, I find every piece of myself and greet it
I've heard this is how self-love begins.

RE: Frost

Roads disingenuous in their unraveling
I will tell you of all the differences it made
Through the concrete that cemented you in poverty
Words tethered between each step
Follow my lead as I step into a poem
I look to the sky, sinking into everything I know; I am a million reasons hoping for the same result
Different shades of light define horizons
The skin that is learning to forget and receive
A bind that continues to intertwine
The conversation between stillness and noise
A pleasure that says, let's disappear
The fervent discourse at the bottom of the bottle
The only thing more difficult than leaving home is knowing you can't return.
Still, I am a million reasons that continue. I tell myself you must learn to forgive.
The trail is narrow. You cannot carry it all.
Where I go, you'll find what I leave, and that is what makes all the difference.

Generational Trauma

Decades of shame wrinkle with regret
Prayers exist as superstitions
Avoiding reflections in the dark, as if protection is something
    that veers with eye contact
Anything to salvage our bloodline
The grandmothers kneading flour, who fold with impelled
    fingers, have a point.
With enough pressure,
Love transcending generations can outlive even the worst hurt.

Raymi

We wait for the hymn that grows among the weeds
That moves through us in spasms
In the current that sweeps through our bodies when we loosen
    the metal door
Laughter resembling petals crackling in death
Flowing through us, finding meaning in the decay
Softness nurtures best in communion
We learn the best of each other
Keep stories from the past safe in our fate
Holding details close before they can fade
Everything we've lived is safe to be free. My fingertips glide into
    your perspective.
You smell of warmth and taste of earth
I think my ancestors sent you to me.

The Odds

He had a 10% chance of survival
Letting the odds linger at his bedside
Fluorescent lighting fluttering a countdown
To survive this
He thought, I'll be damned
To live a life more like a libation
She gripped his hand and held space for a memory to form. The
   sun, peering through the stained glass window the day he
   married her
A light that entered as an awareness
The certainty of the soul, the idea of flesh
The seams of our history, aligned to this moment
I've lived, he thought.
Some say it was luck; others say it was the surgery
He believes survival is an intimate practice
The way you love is the way you survive
A devotion, a surrender you never wake.

I Come from Storytellers

From the aunts who gossip and comment on waistlines
The uncles who imagine a world where they do not have to
   work twelve-hour shifts to make ends meet
The grandparents who tell you of worlds that no longer exist
The parents who describe their dreams for their children as
   doctors, lawyers, and everything in between
The stories that go down generations
Some are cautionary tales, and some offer hope. I gather my
   senses and give them each a purpose
I become a theory full of possibilities
Words undress as they give meaning to spirituality
Fermented talcum powder and soil disguise as air
Burial grounds of someone else's wishes dwell beneath the
   creative process
Phases outgrow each other to outline truths
Growth is a guide, an unearthing of generational wisdom.

New Year's Eve

On New Year's Eve, I watched the countdown, ate my grapes,
    and had lentils in my pocket to symbolize wealth in the
    New Year.
The idea of another year, like light breaking through a polarized
    window
In strains of what it means

My parents are aging.
As if the cancer scare was not enough
As I deciphered resolutions that honored the New Year
I looked at their life—ripened persistence that found its finish
    line. The quest that began in yawning waters, memories
    sealed in floating reflections
A loose clarity absorbed features
A goal symbolized by two cartons of milk in the fridge

They will always be my most remarkable love story
And years can chime in and convince me otherwise
Convince me convictions comes in doses
I let the New Year enter—a privilege untied
To be alive, beneath their eyes
The realization of life.

Grieving the Living

I have been hoping death treats you kindly. That the prayers
 that hurt to remember will drift off
Wage resistance from the crumbling foundation
Death translucent in its pursuit
That morphine, tormenting the harmony of the land
A home reclaiming the earth
Will speckle light in your peripheral
The body reminiscing on life
I contemplate my sanity as I hope you go sooner. Borrowed
 quotes tell me grief has already begun.
Survive the plague, outsmart the depression, suppress the
 hunger, vilify the thirst. I want to honor the rest as well.
The calloused hands that held empathy
The jokes you were proud of
The expressions that were never afraid of wrinkles
Desires that veiled us into tomorrow
Somewhere, someone is making a list of changes for their life,
 deconstructing the past for a better future.
Others are on a first date, admiring the space between each
 gaze. Some write their first poem, their first script, their first
 song. I take comfort in knowing you experienced life like
 this.
If   hospice   is   anything   other   than   letting
 go,   it   is   learning   what   to   hold.

Herlinda

I know a language only in carvings.
Carved in a sky only visible in recollections.
I look down at my arms and process shame for thinking my
    skin was ever an insult.
Waraq. I come home to you in meditation.
I raise survival in your reflection. Tend moons to the surface.
    Name plants in your tribute, I see your blood
    for what it is.
The starch of the night, earth adjusting to hues. The gravel
    following a morning commute.
Tasseled light making an entrance, a home of this country. I
    grieve patriotism for what it is.
Loving a mother I have no memory of.

In Time

The wind, in sync with my patience.
I test the weight of my body on each leg.
The attraction is tense between my soaked socks and the grass.
    The smushed lilies on the sidewalk are raising the stakes.
The dogs are barking next door, a comfort. I am still here. I pry
    my eyes up, belted to uphold
To trust.
The universe is scaling time without a care.
The scuffed second-hand furniture, the coffee beans we searched
    three different stores for
The entry-level jobs we imagined leaving.
The quotes we swore by and shared over dinner.
I purposefully ate too fast on our first date to not miss a word.
    The first picture we ever hung was crooked, and we jokingly
    blamed it on the architecture.
I now understand the older man in Houston observing life from
    his porch.
Be still.
The world is reveling.

Llamellín

The saint that followed me to Los Angeles would be at rest
If I coiled lands from my veins, pulverized heat leading the way
Found meaning in the stature of the mountains
The light of little weight
Rising from the mudslide that buried our history
The living memory of this land, my lungs react out of habit
The grandmother I never knew continues to speak through
    reason
Wherever I follow, I am never alone.

Lessons from the Shaman in Cusco

He tells me words frayed upon words
Radiating truths that evolve tradition
Be grateful not for your life but for all life
I let my mind ferment
Glide with silence
Gratitude is not a thing that happens when spoken into
    existence
My being performing a balance
I tell him I will change and do better
I will bask in generational gifts
As we walk down the mountains, peaks of white, defying heat
Shoes scuffle with dirt that seeks uncertainty
He walks over to wash his hand by the river
As he thanks the water for its purpose
I realize
Gratitude is something you feel, the extraordinary that happens
    when you choose to belong.

A Birth

I ask the ancestors, tell me, is this faith? A correlation between
    love and peace
The current that drifts into reconciliation over and over until
    there is no distinction
A bind held by my very limbs
I now understand how land becomes holy
How sacredness is pulled from the scorch
How in the debris there are remnants of belief
How gratitude is the birthplace of intimacy
How *will* unearthed, is living
You are the offspring of all our prayers
With you, hope is infinite.

Descriptions

I only know love in relation to what my body responds to.
Slight compressions from the sun as I step in and out of the
    shade
Eyelashes that spend the entire day finding each other
The brash sand wrapping around my body almost immediately
The timidness of my hair as it considers how to part
    comfortably
How to lash out when the wind acts out of character
The fullness in my breath when I feel content
Edging my lungs to sanity
I refer to this feeling as *enough*. Every touch is a release of need.
    An instinct is professing a home.

The New Age

I watched a documentary about a man from Kansas embarking on an ayahuasca journey to heal his depression. I carried my sigh till the end: another documentary from a perspective that is not ours. All I have ever wanted is for my people to be seen.

Like the shaman who only spoke Quechua that cracked a smile when I said the name of my grandparents' hometown.
The children with the pulp of the land under their fingernails digging into a granadilla.
The street artist using acrylics to conjure worlds.
The couple finding their way around the city as they exit from each other.
The woman cooped in her street cart, excited to see a customer. The parents half-sinking into the grass, watching their children run from corner to corner.
The elderly man budding enthusiastically, finding someone to speak to about the mundane.
The healer at the mercado spoiling the desperate with blessings. The laughter of the taxi drivers drowning the sirens of the city.
The tilted hope adjusting to each person in the middle of prayer.

At the end of the documentary, the man found peace. I turned off the TV, sat with those emotions, and thought that despite everything my people went through, they still chose to heal the world.

How to Re-frame the Breakup

If the edge of the couch allows me, if the rigid carpet welcomes my pacing at midnight, if the wind breaking in from the cracked window takes a step back, if I can come into this room and recall when it was over. I come home hollow with my voice attached to the cracks and moans. We all want to believe we can love the rage out of someone. Mediate with their trauma, and allow an exit plan to become within reach. I imagine a world where he learned less from his father. Without the deceptions his mother glossed on her lips, the violence she endured to not be alone in this country. I imagine he was peacefully asleep when his father came home drunk, preying on drywall and her throat. A world where his mother packed her bags, took him in the car, and never looked back. That there was day she caught his hands in mid-air, held them in place, and taught him, he could do more with his fists. I imagine a world where he learned to be gentle; a burn from touching the stove was treated with raw honey and silly rhymes. A world where he spent more time enunciating his feelings to the soft brim of the sunset. A world where he learned to sit in with the roar of his thoughts and made something of the chaos. Made art, made hope. A world where he dictated his prayers out loud. A world where he believed forgiveness had substance. I imagine a life where the end of us wasn't life or death; instead, we let each other go. Made coffee with new lovers. Discovered new ways to express affection. Spelled out dreams neither of us would ever know. We would have grieved the loss of each other and moved on. Instead, the mild wind entering the room exposes something else. The want is freed of expectations. I am at mercy with healing.

Amar

Cuando la oscuridad se despeja
Y viene la luz en todo su gracia
Cada *mi amor* y *mi vida*
Se convierten en una conclusión eterna
Un entendimiento entre la semilla y la raíz
La historia de amor, las lenguas que sobrevivieron porque
    aprendieron a expresarse con tacto
Y nosotros existimos en las conversaciones enredadas entre las
    sabanas
Y tú eres las páginas que pasaré el resto de mi vida escribiendo
Y la última página dirá
Las vidas que nuestros padres dejaron para traernos juntos
Valió la peña
Y peña's había en cantidad
Pero hoy llenemos los rincones del cuarto con lo esperanza que
    ya acabo la guerra.

Choice

I tell you, I choose you in every sense
To love one of my own
Our hips are aligned to the same burned sunset our ancestors
 baked. It is possible to leave reminders
To leave a piece of our day and leave it to become.
I've left my reservations in the shadow of our facial features. The
 diluted promises we once guarded
Hardened to something tangible, something permanent.
The home we create is an isle of everything we've ever been. I
 believe this is loving in your native tongue
Every cell is a recognition.

The Most Important

I want to believe in unscathed freedom
The kind that pinches your skin
The one borrowing light from your conviction
The type of freedom that belongs to the rhythm
The release of doubt. Anxiety. Depression.
The wholeness that is associated with accepting every thought.
    As time bridges wisdom
I come correct of life. Of hope. A child is not the first life we
    carry.
As reflections part ways with distance
I take the only perspective I've ever had.
The one that pauses to admire the new houseplant
The one that thanked God after being safe after the car accident
The one that learned grief is how the body shows compassion
The palpable words I whispered the first night we fell asleep
    together
This life is caught in the wrinkles of my dress. This life I carry
    beneath the skin that adjusts to the sun.
The woven freedom that attests to the voice that has finally
    spoke up.

All the Best

I'll give you the days that belong to the best of me.
A rehearsal of words I know will urge a sunrise.
As if *best* can be defined by anything or anyone
I'll look for the scars on the hardwood floor
The water stains on the bathroom mirror
The spilled salt scattered on the kitchen counter
All the signs of living to understand this suspicion. The dying
    grief. The living need to be loved.
My mourning and my joy will come along
Like the sufficient hope that carried me here
Like the spring doorstop that always steps in to help
If best belongs in the now, then I'll catch you practicing a
    glance during commercial breaks
A look pressing on the outskirt of our story
The wonder of it all is how I know. I always knew.

History

Before Túpac Amaru was a commodity and led the largest uprising against the Spanish, legend has it that his final words before being killed by the Spanish were, "I will return, and I will be millions." My mom used to tell me when they say "te sale tu Indio," it refers back to that. Looking inward, I can find manifestationlike curtains amassing, leaving smokelike skies. They call it pollution when they want to be honest. Even through the headers of the mountains, you can glimpse the past. The formations that drunkenly swept so many under.

The food is cooking underground for a reason. Clusters of the earth are parting ways with its breath. To be a million guesses when they want to play, Let Me Guess Your Ethnicity. I allow my chin to rest on my shoulder, reviewing my side profile. "Go on," I say. The pauses dictate a plan. The wildfires may have something to say. When the trees burn to the ground, their ashes nourish the next generation of trees. Not all ash corrupts the lungs. Perhaps that is where this deep desire to survive despite it all comes from. We are millions.

Behind the Apartment

The little girl that defended her gulp, living in the dingbat
    apartment in Canoga Park
Curls roughed up by the inkling of the dumpster she excavated
    every weekend
If you asked her, she never knew she was poor
There was value in the dumpster
The Barbies with missing limbs
The books with scuffed edges and wrinkled pages
The teddy bears with missing buttons and coffee stains
Her dad, on the other hand
Carried the guilt under his eyes
A tension bridged what he could give and what he couldn't
As if putting food on the table wasn't hard enough
A loosened grief widened to last a little every day
Still, he promised her the canyons bleeding into their home
Speak of the drought, speak of the rain
Speak of life dividing alms and wealth
What I give you will last a lifetime, and what I can't, you'll find
    a way to make last
If you ask her, she did not know she was poor, but she did know
        the most damaged, the most disrupted,
  always   made   you   feel   the   most.

Leaning

Tousled hair embracing the rail of the bed,
Another thing I refuse to cut short
To live in the sigh, the yearning
To make something of the light encroaching through the blinds,
    I've left my devotion slanted somewhere to fit in.
The intimacy left of the skin communicating.
To enunciate the dreams I have never shared until now,
The isolation of denying oneself
The loathing staving off the shelf life of ambition
Eventually, the rest you desperately lures every organ. I've given
    my dreams a witness.
Immersed in the sockets of your observations, I count on ease.

Effort

When words and meanings do not meet
The silence is what becomes of me after I've exhausted all my dignity
When intrusive thoughts become lucid
When fear is inconsolable
Insecurities begin to sound more like affirmations
Helplessly shoveling whatever hope I have between me and the bathroom cabinet.
My mind will say we will try again tomorrow
Collect all the thoughts spilled
The white tablecloth will stretch its fingers across the entire table
Recoil the doubt clinging to the dipping vein when I bend my wrist back
When the sun rises, we will make amends.

Advice

Bravery begins with belief
With pulling the earth apart, separating prayers from truths

Sometimes the only truth
that exists is that
you need that prayer

Belief comes around
and does not recognize
the shutter of your eyes
The consistency of your skin
a visceral connection
of what has always been

The vibration of your voice
when you say
I'll try again tomorrow

I've seen bravery
The first *I love you*
The job two-thousand miles away
The kiss on the forehead when the cancer is terminal
The wife who sold her wedding ring for the plane ticket
The dad who built the crib before he heard the first cry
The sister who became the first

What is bravery but a home,
an act of solidarity
The resting place
of everything I've survived.

ACKNOWLEDGMENTS

I began writing poetry at the age of five. At the time, it seemed like a creative outlet I would dive into whenever the night permitted—a space I could enter without shame or judgment. All of my thoughts and dreams filled pages of spiral notebooks.

I owe it to that little girl, every dream I've conjured, every poem, every word. If I could ever go back in time, I would thank her. Tell her about the slither of the night that rolled away this morning and revealed the most beautiful sunrise. I would tell her she is the reason I am fearless. She is why I've never been afraid to try again and again. I would say to her if each moment were a verse, every book would lie in defeat. That is how great your story will be. Thank you.

www.ingramcontent.com/pod-product-compliance
Lightning Source LLC
Chambersburg PA
CBHW060539080526
44586CB00012B/798